Flavors of Italy

The Ultimate Alfredo Fotuccini Cookbook

FLAVORS OF ITALY

First edition. January 9, 2024.

ISBN: 979-8224502202

Written by Jose Maria.

Table of Contents

Jose Maria

❖ Introduction

A. Brief History and Origin of Alfredo Fotuccini

Alfredo Fotuccini, a beloved Italian culinary masterpiece, traces its roots back to early 20th-century Rome. The dish was originally known as "Fettuccine Alfredo" and was created by Alfredo di Lelio, a restaurateur. Legend has it that Alfredo concocted this iconic pasta dish in the 1920s as a gesture to comfort and nourish his pregnant wife. The simple yet luxurious combination of butter, cream, and Parmesan became an instant sensation, captivating the hearts and palates of locals and visitors alike.

B. The Allure of Alfredo Fotuccini in Italian Cuisine

Alfredo Fotuccini holds a special place in the tapestry of Italian cuisine, representing the epitome of indulgence and elegance. Its rich, velvety sauce clings to the strands of pasta, creating a symphony of flavors that dance on the taste buds. The dish perfectly encapsulates the Italian approach to culinary artistry—celebrating the quality of ingredients through uncomplicated yet sophisticated preparations. Alfredo Fotuccini is not just a meal; it's a culinary experience that transcends time, making it a staple on tables across Italy and around the world.

C. Overview of the Cookbook's Purpose and Structure

Welcome to "Flavors of Italy: The Ultimate Alfredo Fotuccini Cookbook," where we embark on a journey to explore the diverse dimensions of this classic dish. This cookbook aims to demystify the art of creating Alfredo Fotuccini in all its glory, from the traditional recipe that started it all to innovative variations that push culinary boundaries.

Structured to be a comprehensive guide, this cookbook is divided into sections that cater to different tastes and preferences. Whether you're a purist longing for the authentic flavors or an adventurous cook seeking creative twists, you'll find something delightful within these pages. Alongside the recipes, we delve into the history, share kitchen essentials, and offer expert tips to ensure your Alfredo Fotuccini is nothing short of perfection.

Get ready to unleash your inner Italian chef as we explore the enchanting world of Alfredo Fotuccini—one recipe at a time. Buon Appetito!

Chapter (1) Kitchen Essentials

A. Tools and Equipment for Preparing Alfredo Fotuccini

Large Pot:

Essential for cooking the Fotuccini pasta to perfection. Ensure it is spacious enough to avoid overcrowding.

Saucepan:

Ideal for preparing the Alfredo sauce. Choose a heavy-bottomed saucepan to prevent burning and ensure even heating.

Whisk or Wooden Spoon:

Necessary for stirring the Alfredo sauce. A whisk helps achieve a smooth consistency, while a wooden spoon is excellent for gentle stirring.

Colander:

Used for draining the cooked pasta. Make sure it has fine holes to prevent the pasta from slipping through.

Cheese Grater:

To grate fresh Parmesan cheese. Opt for a fine grater for a melt-in-your-mouth texture.

Pasta Server or Tongs:

Useful for lifting and serving the cooked Fotuccini without damaging the strands.

Measuring Cups and Spoons:

Ensure accurate measurements for the sauce ingredients.

B. Ingredients Guide - Selecting the Finest Components

Fotuccini Pasta:

Opt for high-quality, durum wheat Fotuccini for an authentic taste and texture.

Parmesan Cheese:

Choose freshly grated Parmesan for maximum flavor. Avoid pre-packaged, pre-shredded varieties for better results.

Heavy Cream:

Use high-fat content heavy cream for a rich and creamy sauce.

Unsalted Butter:

Select unsalted butter to control the saltiness of the dish.

Salt and Pepper:

Preferably use freshly ground black pepper for enhanced flavor.

C. Tips for Achieving the Perfect Alfredo Fotuccini Consistency

Temperature Control:

Keep the heat medium-low when preparing the sauce to avoid curdling or separation.

Constant Stirring:

Stir the sauce continuously to ensure even melting of the cheese and a smooth texture.

Use Fresh Ingredients:

Opt for fresh Parmesan and high-quality cream for the best flavor and consistency.

Timing is Key:

Cook the pasta al dente, and time its readiness to coincide with the completion of the sauce for a perfect marriage of flavors and textures.

Reserve Pasta Water:

Before draining the pasta, reserve a cup of the cooking water. Adding a splash to the sauce can help adjust its consistency.

Serve Immediately:

Alfredo Fotuccini is best enjoyed immediately after preparation. The pasta tends to absorb the sauce over time, so serve promptly for optimal creaminess.

With these kitchen essentials and expert tips, you're well-equipped to embark on your Alfredo Fotuccini culinary adventure. Enjoy the process and savor the results!

Chapter (2) Classic Alfredo Fotuccini Recipes

A. Traditional Alfredo Fotuccini with Parmesan and Cream

1. Step-by-Step Preparation Guide:

Ingredients:

- 1 lb Fotuccini pasta
- 1 cup heavy cream
- 1 cup grated Parmesan cheese
- 1/2 cup unsalted butter
- Salt and pepper to taste
- Fresh parsley for garnish

Instructions:

1. Cook Fotuccini pasta according to package instructions. Drain and set aside.
2. In a saucepan over medium heat, melt the butter.
3. Pour in the heavy cream, stirring continuously to combine.
4. Gradually add the grated Parmesan cheese, stirring until the sauce is smooth.
5. Season with salt and pepper to taste. Continue stirring until the sauce thickens.
6. Toss the cooked Fotuccini pasta into the Alfredo sauce, ensuring an even coating.
7. Garnish with fresh parsley and serve immediately.

2. Tips for Achieving a Velvety Sauce:

- Use room temperature heavy cream and butter for faster and smoother blending.

- Add Parmesan gradually, allowing each addition to melt before adding more.
- Adjust heat as needed; low to medium heat prevents the sauce from breaking or becoming too thin.

B. Chicken Alfredo Fotuccini
1. Adding Protein to the Classic Dish:
Ingredients:

- 1 lb Fotuccini pasta
- 1 cup heavy cream
- 1 cup grated Parmesan cheese
- 1/2 cup unsalted butter
- Salt and pepper to taste
- Fresh parsley for garnish
- 1 lb chicken breast, sliced and cooked

Instructions:

1. Follow the steps for the Traditional Alfredo Fotuccini recipe.
2. Add cooked chicken slices to the Alfredo sauce and pasta before tossing.
3. Ensure the chicken is evenly distributed throughout the dish.
4. Garnish with fresh parsley and serve.

2. Flavor Variations and Seasoning Suggestions:

- Enhance the chicken with Italian herbs like basil, oregano, and thyme during cooking.
- For a hint of heat, add a pinch of red pepper flakes to the Alfredo sauce.

- Experiment with different cheese blends, such as adding a touch of mozzarella for extra creaminess.

C. Shrimp and Spinach Alfredo Fotuccini
1. Incorporating Seafood and Greens:
Ingredients:

- 1 lb Fotuccini pasta
- 1 cup heavy cream
- 1 cup grated Parmesan cheese
- 1/2 cup unsalted butter
- Salt and pepper to taste
- Fresh parsley for garnish
- 1 lb shrimp, peeled and deveined
- 2 cups fresh spinach, washed and chopped

Instructions:

1. Prepare the Alfredo sauce following the Traditional Alfredo Fotuccini recipe.
2. In a separate pan, sauté shrimp until pink and opaque. Set aside.
3. Add chopped spinach to the Alfredo sauce during the last minute of cooking.
4. Toss the cooked Fotuccini pasta with the Alfredo sauce, shrimp, and spinach.
5. Garnish with fresh parsley and serve promptly.

2. Balancing Flavors for a Delightful Combination:

- Season shrimp with garlic, lemon, and a touch of paprika for depth of flavor.
- Ensure spinach is added towards the end to retain its vibrant color and freshness.
- Adjust seasoning with salt and pepper to harmonize the flavors

of seafood and greens.

Chapter (3) Creative Alfredo Fotuccini Variations

A. Broccoli and Sun-Dried Tomato Alfredo Fotuccini
1. Introducing Vegetables and Bold Flavors:
Ingredients:

- 1 lb Fotuccini pasta
- 1 cup heavy cream
- 1 cup grated Parmesan cheese
- 1/2 cup unsalted butter
- Salt and pepper to taste
- Fresh parsley for garnish
- 2 cups broccoli florets, blanched
- 1/2 cup sun-dried tomatoes, julienned

Instructions:

1. Follow the Traditional Alfredo Fotuccini recipe to prepare the base sauce.
2. Add blanched broccoli florets and julienned sun-dried tomatoes to the Alfredo sauce.
3. Toss the cooked Fotuccini pasta into the sauce, ensuring even distribution of vegetables.
4. Garnish with fresh parsley and serve for a vibrant and flavorful variation.

2. Texture Contrasts for a Well-Rounded Dish:

- Blanch broccoli until tender-crisp for a delightful texture contrast.
- Sun-dried tomatoes add a chewy and tangy element, enhancing the overall complexity of the dish.

B. Mushroom and Truffle Oil Alfredo Fotuccini
1. Elevating the Dish with Earthy Flavors:
Ingredients:

- 1 lb Fotuccini pasta
- 1 cup heavy cream
- 1 cup grated Parmesan cheese
- 1/2 cup unsalted butter
- Salt and pepper to taste
- Fresh parsley for garnish
- 1 cup assorted mushrooms (such as cremini, shiitake), sliced
- Truffle oil for drizzling

Instructions:

1. Prepare the Traditional Alfredo Fotuccini sauce as directed.
2. In a separate pan, sauté sliced mushrooms until golden brown.
3. Toss the cooked Fotuccini pasta with the Alfredo sauce and sautéed mushrooms.
4. Drizzle truffle oil over the dish before serving for an indulgent touch.
5. Garnish with fresh parsley and enjoy the rich, earthy flavors.

2. Choosing the Right Mushrooms for Depth of Taste:

- Combine different mushroom varieties for a nuanced flavor

profile.

- Sauté mushrooms until they release their moisture and develop a golden color for enhanced taste.

C. Spinach and Artichoke Alfredo Fotuccini
1. Fusing Classic Italian Ingredients:
Ingredients:

- 1 lb Fotuccini pasta
- 1 cup heavy cream
- 1 cup grated Parmesan cheese
- 1/2 cup unsalted butter
- Salt and pepper to taste
- Fresh parsley for garnish
- 2 cups fresh spinach, chopped
- 1 cup artichoke hearts, drained and chopped

Instructions:

1. Follow the steps to prepare the Traditional Alfredo Fotuccini sauce.
2. Add chopped spinach and artichoke hearts to the Alfredo sauce, allowing them to wilt and soften.
3. Toss the cooked Fotuccini pasta in the sauce until well-coated.
4. Garnish with fresh parsley and serve for a delightful fusion of classic Italian flavors.

2. Achieving a Harmonious Blend of Flavors:

- Fresh spinach brings a vibrant, earthy taste, while artichoke hearts add a mild, slightly tangy note.
- Ensure artichoke hearts are well-drained to prevent excess

moisture in the sauce.

Chapter (4) Healthier Alfredo Fotuccini Options

A. Cauliflower Alfredo Fotuccini

1. A Lighter, Vegetable-Based Alternative:

Ingredients:

- 1 lb Fotuccini pasta
- 1 medium cauliflower, cut into florets
- 1 cup vegetable broth
- 1/2 cup unsweetened almond milk
- 1/4 cup nutritional yeast
- 2 cloves garlic, minced
- 2 tablespoons olive oil
- Salt and pepper to taste
- Fresh parsley for garnish

Instructions:

1. Cook Fotuccini pasta according to package instructions. Drain and set aside.
2. Steam cauliflower florets until tender.
3. In a blender, combine steamed cauliflower, vegetable broth, almond milk, nutritional yeast, minced garlic, and olive oil. Blend until smooth.
4. Season the cauliflower Alfredo sauce with salt and pepper to taste.
5. Toss the cooked Fotuccini pasta in the cauliflower Alfredo sauce until well-coated.
6. Garnish with fresh parsley and serve for a lighter twist on the classic dish.

2. Tips for Maintaining Creaminess Without Heavy Ingredients:

- Ensure cauliflower is fully cooked and tender to achieve a velvety texture in the sauce.
- Adjust the consistency by adding more vegetable broth or almond milk as needed.
- Nutritional yeast adds a cheesy flavor without the heaviness of traditional cheese.

B. Whole Wheat Alfredo Fotuccini

1. Incorporating Whole Grains for Added Nutrition:

Ingredients:

- 1 lb whole wheat Fotuccini pasta
- 1 cup heavy cream
- 1 cup grated Parmesan cheese
- 1/2 cup unsalted butter
- Salt and pepper to taste
- Fresh parsley for garnish

Instructions:

1. Cook whole wheat Fotuccini pasta according to package instructions. Drain and set aside.
2. In a saucepan over medium heat, melt the butter.
3. Pour in the heavy cream, stirring continuously to combine.
4. Gradually add the grated Parmesan cheese, stirring until the sauce is smooth.
5. Season with salt and pepper to taste. Continue stirring until the sauce thickens.
6. Toss the cooked whole wheat Fotuccini pasta into the Alfredo sauce, ensuring an even coating.
7. Garnish with fresh parsley and serve immediately.

2. Flavor Adjustments to Complement the Heartier Pasta:

- The nutty flavor of whole wheat pairs well with the richness of the Alfredo sauce.
- Consider adding a touch more seasoning to balance the heartier taste of whole wheat pasta.
- Fresh herbs like thyme or rosemary can enhance the overall flavor profile.

Chapter (5) Sides and Complements

A. Garlic Breadsticks

1. A Classic Accompaniment to Alfredo Fotuccini:

Ingredients:

- 1 lb pizza dough (store-bought or homemade)
- 1/2 cup unsalted butter, melted
- 3 cloves garlic, minced
- 2 tablespoons fresh parsley, finely chopped
- Salt to taste

Instructions:

1. Preheat the oven according to the pizza dough package instructions or your homemade recipe.
2. Roll out the pizza dough into a rectangular shape.
3. In a bowl, mix melted butter, minced garlic, chopped parsley, and a pinch of salt.
4. Brush the garlic butter mixture evenly over the rolled-out dough.
5. Cut the dough into strips to form breadsticks.
6. Place the breadsticks on a baking sheet and bake according to the pizza dough instructions until golden brown.
7. Serve warm alongside Alfredo Fotuccini for a classic and comforting combination.

2. Homemade Garlic Butter for an Extra Touch:

- Adjust the intensity of garlic to your preference for a personalized flavor profile.
- Sprinkle a little extra Parmesan or a blend of Italian herbs on top of the garlic butter for added richness.

B. Caesar Salad with Homemade Dressing
1. Perfectly Pairing Greens with the Rich Pasta Dish:
Ingredients:

- 1 head romaine lettuce, washed and torn into bite-sized pieces
- 1 cup croutons
- 1/2 cup shaved Parmesan cheese
- Caesar dressing (see recipe below)
- Freshly ground black pepper to taste
- Lemon wedges for serving

Instructions:

- In a large bowl, combine romaine lettuce, croutons, and shaved Parmesan cheese.
- Drizzle Caesar dressing over the salad and toss until evenly coated.
- Serve the Caesar salad alongside a plate of Alfredo Fotuccini.
- Garnish with additional Parmesan and freshly ground black pepper.
- Squeeze lemon wedges over the salad for a refreshing touch.

2. Crafting a Caesar Dressing that Enhances the Meal:
Ingredients:

- 1/2 cup mayonnaise
- 2 tablespoons Dijon mustard
- 2 cloves garlic, minced
- 2 anchovy fillets, minced (optional)
- 1 tablespoon Worcestershire sauce
- 1 tablespoon red wine vinegar
- 1/2 cup grated Parmesan cheese
- Salt and black pepper to taste
- 1/2 cup extra-virgin olive oil

Instructions:

1. In a bowl, whisk together mayonnaise, Dijon mustard, minced garlic, anchovies (if using), Worcestershire sauce, red wine vinegar, Parmesan cheese, salt, and black pepper.
2. Slowly drizzle in the olive oil while whisking continuously to emulsify the dressing.
3. Adjust salt and pepper according to taste.
4. Refrigerate the dressing until ready to use.
5. Shake or whisk the dressing before pouring over the salad.

Pairing Caesar salad with Alfredo Fotuccini creates a well-rounded meal with contrasting textures and flavors. Enjoy the vibrant freshness of the salad alongside the indulgent richness of the pasta dish.

Chapter (6) Tips for Perfecting Alfredo Fotuccini

A. Troubleshooting Common Issues

Sauce Separation:

Issue: If the sauce appears to separate, it may be due to high heat or overcooking.

Solution: Lower the heat and stir consistently. If the sauce does separate, a splash of cold cream while stirring can help re-emulsify it.

Sauce Too Thick:

Issue: The Alfredo sauce may become too thick.

Solution: Adjust the consistency by adding a bit of reserved pasta water, chicken broth, or milk until the desired thickness is achieved.

Pasta Overcooking:

Issue: Overcooked pasta can lead to a mushy texture.

Solution: Cook pasta al dente, and time it carefully. Immediately drain and toss it in the sauce to prevent further cooking.

Cheese Clumping:

Issue: Cheese may clump if added too quickly or without proper stirring.

Solution: Gradually add cheese while stirring continuously. Consider grating the cheese finer for smoother integration.

Sauce Too Thin:

Issue: If the sauce is too thin, it might need more time to simmer.

Solution: Simmer the sauce over low heat while stirring until it reaches the desired thickness.

B. Storing and Reheating Leftovers

Storing Leftovers:

Allow leftovers to cool to room temperature before refrigerating.

Store Alfredo Fotuccini in an airtight container in the refrigerator for up to 2-3 days.

Reheating:

Gently reheat leftovers in a saucepan over low heat to prevent the sauce from breaking.

Add a splash of cream or milk while reheating to restore creaminess.

Alternatively, reheat in the microwave at 50% power, stirring at intervals.

Refreshing Pasta:

Toss reheated pasta with a touch of olive oil or additional Alfredo sauce for a fresher taste.

C. Hosting an Alfredo Fotuccini-Themed Dinner Party

Invitations:

Set the tone with invitations that evoke the richness and warmth of Italian cuisine. Consider using images of Alfredo Fotuccini or a rustic Italian backdrop.

Decor:

Create a cozy, Italian-inspired atmosphere with red and white checkered tablecloths, candlelight, and rustic tableware.

Menu Variety:

Offer a variety of Alfredo Fotuccini options, including classics and creative variations, catering to different preferences.

Appetizers:

Serve Italian appetizers like bruschetta, antipasto platters, or stuffed mushrooms to kick off the meal.

Wine Pairing:

Provide a selection of Italian wines such as Chardonnay or Pinot Grigio to complement the richness of the Alfredo Fotuccini.

Desserts:

End the evening with classic Italian desserts like Tiramisu or cannoli for a sweet finale.

Music Playlist:

Set the mood with a playlist featuring classic Italian tunes or instrumental music for a sophisticated ambiance.

Interactive Elements:

Consider having a pasta bar where guests can customize their Alfredo Fotuccini with various toppings and ingredients.

Cooking Demonstration:

If space allows, host a cooking demonstration to showcase the art of preparing Alfredo Fotuccini.

Favors:

Send guests home with small jars of homemade Alfredo sauce, pasta, or Italian-themed goodies as a delightful party favor.

Remember to enjoy the process of creating an authentic Italian experience for your guests, filled with delicious food, good company, and the enchanting aroma of Alfredo Fotuccini. Buon Appetito!

Chapter (7) International Alfredo Fusion

A. Asian-Inspired Alfredo Fotuccini with Sesame and Bok Choy

   1. Infusing Asian Flavors into the Classic Italian Dish:

Ingredients:

- 1 lb Fotuccini pasta
- 1 cup heavy cream
- 1 cup grated Parmesan cheese
- 1/2 cup unsalted butter
- Salt and pepper to taste
- Fresh parsley for garnish
- 2 cups bok choy, chopped
- 2 tablespoons soy sauce
- 1 tablespoon sesame oil
- 2 teaspoons ginger, minced
- 2 cloves garlic, minced
- 1 tablespoon toasted sesame seeds

Instructions:

1. Cook Fotuccini pasta according to package instructions. Drain and set aside.
2. In a saucepan over medium heat, melt the butter.
3. Add minced ginger and garlic, sautéing until fragrant.
4. Pour in the heavy cream, stirring continuously to combine.
5. Gradually add the grated Parmesan cheese, soy sauce, and sesame oil, continuing to stir until the sauce is smooth.
6. Season with salt and pepper to taste. Adjust soy sauce and sesame oil if needed for balance.
7. Toss the cooked Fotuccini pasta into the Alfredo sauce.
8. In a separate pan, stir-fry chopped bok choy until tender-crisp.

9. Add the bok choy to the Alfredo Fotuccini and toss until well-coated.

10. Garnish with toasted sesame seeds and fresh parsley before serving.

2. Balancing Umami and Creaminess:

- Adjust the ratio of soy sauce and sesame oil to achieve the desired level of umami and richness.
- Toasted sesame seeds add a nutty flavor and an appealing crunch, providing a delightful contrast to the creamy pasta.

This Asian-inspired Alfredo Fotuccini offers a unique fusion of flavors, marrying the velvety richness of the classic Italian dish with the umami notes of soy sauce, sesame, and the crisp freshness of bok choy. Enjoy this international twist on a beloved favorite!

Chapter (8) Seasonal Alfredo Delights

A. Summer Garden Alfredo Fotuccini with Fresh Tomatoes and Basil
1. Highlighting Seasonal Produce for a Vibrant Twist:
Ingredients:

- 1 lb Fotuccini pasta
- 1 cup heavy cream
- 1 cup grated Parmesan cheese
- 1/2 cup unsalted butter
- Salt and pepper to taste
- Fresh parsley for garnish
- 2 cups fresh tomatoes, diced
- 1/2 cup cherry tomatoes, halved
- 1/2 cup fresh basil leaves, torn
- 2 cloves garlic, minced
- 1 tablespoon olive oil

Instructions:

1. Cook Fotuccini pasta according to package instructions. Drain and set aside.
2. In a saucepan over medium heat, melt the butter and add minced garlic. Sauté until fragrant.
3. Pour in the heavy cream, stirring continuously to combine.
4. Gradually add the grated Parmesan cheese, stirring until the sauce is smooth.
5. Season with salt and pepper to taste. Continue stirring until the sauce thickens.
6. Toss the cooked Fotuccini pasta into the Alfredo sauce.
7. In a separate pan, heat olive oil and add diced fresh tomatoes. Sauté until slightly softened.

8. Add halved cherry tomatoes to the pan and cook briefly, maintaining their freshness.
9. Mix the sautéed tomatoes with the Alfredo Fotuccini.
10. Just before serving, sprinkle torn fresh basil leaves over the pasta.
11. Garnish with fresh parsley and serve immediately.

2. Incorporating Herbs for a Burst of Freshness:

- Add fresh basil at the last moment to preserve its aromatic flavor.
- Adjust the garlic and Parmesan levels to allow the sweetness of the summer tomatoes and the brightness of basil to shine through.

Celebrate the flavors of summer with this garden-inspired Alfredo Fotuccini, featuring the best of the season's produce. The combination of ripe tomatoes and fragrant basil elevates this dish to a delightful seasonal delight. Enjoy the taste of summer on your plate!

Chapter (9) Alfredo-Inspired Breakfast Dishes

A. Alfredo Breakfast Scramble with Eggs and Spinach
  1. Transforming the Beloved Pasta into a Morning Delight:
Ingredients:

- 6 large eggs
- 1/2 cup heavy cream
- 1/2 cup grated Parmesan cheese
- 3 tablespoons unsalted butter
- Salt and pepper to taste
- 2 cups fresh spinach, chopped
- 2 cloves garlic, minced
- 1 tablespoon olive oil
- Fresh chives for garnish

Instructions:

1. In a bowl, whisk together eggs, heavy cream, and grated Parmesan cheese. Season with salt and pepper.
2. Heat olive oil and 2 tablespoons of butter in a skillet over medium heat.
3. Add minced garlic and sauté until fragrant.
4. Pour the egg mixture into the skillet, stirring gently.
5. When the eggs start to set, add chopped spinach and continue to stir until the eggs are fully cooked.
6. Adjust seasoning as needed and remove from heat.
7. Melt the remaining tablespoon of butter in the hot skillet and stir it into the eggs for added richness.
8. Garnish with fresh chives before serving.

2. Tips for a Hearty and Satisfying Breakfast:

- Use fresh and high-quality eggs for a richer flavor.
- Adjust the amount of cream and cheese to achieve the desired creaminess.
- Experiment with additional breakfast-friendly ingredients such as diced ham or sautéed mushrooms.

This Alfredo-inspired breakfast scramble transforms the classic pasta dish into a hearty morning delight. The combination of creamy eggs, Parmesan, and vibrant spinach creates a satisfying breakfast that's sure to start your day on a delicious note. Enjoy this unique twist on the traditional Alfredo!

Chapter (10) Vegan Alfredo Alternatives

A. Cashew Cream Alfredo Fotuccini with Roasted Vegetables
    1. Crafting a Dairy-Free, Plant-Based Alfredo Sauce:
Ingredients:

- 1 lb Fotuccini pasta (ensure it's vegan)
- 1 1/2 cups raw cashews, soaked in water for at least 4 hours
- 1 1/2 cups vegetable broth
- 1/4 cup nutritional yeast
- 3 cloves garlic, minced
- 2 tablespoons lemon juice
- 2 tablespoons olive oil
- Salt and pepper to taste
- Fresh parsley for garnish

Instructions:

1. Cook Fotuccini pasta according to package instructions. Drain and set aside.
2. In a blender, combine soaked cashews, vegetable broth, nutritional yeast, minced garlic, lemon juice, olive oil, salt, and pepper.
3. Blend until the mixture is smooth and creamy, adjusting consistency with more vegetable broth if needed.
4. In a saucepan over medium heat, warm the cashew cream mixture, stirring continuously until heated through.
5. Toss the cooked Fotuccini pasta into the cashew cream Alfredo sauce, ensuring an even coating.
6. Garnish with fresh parsley before serving.

2. Enhancing Flavors with Roasted Veggies:

- Select a variety of colorful vegetables such as cherry tomatoes, bell peppers, zucchini, and broccoli for roasting.
- Toss the vegetables in olive oil, salt, and pepper before roasting to enhance their natural flavors.
- Roast the veggies in the oven until they are tender and slightly caramelized, adding a delightful contrast to the creamy Alfredo.

This Cashew Cream Alfredo Fotuccini with Roasted Vegetables offers a delicious and satisfying vegan alternative to the traditional dish. The rich and creamy cashew sauce, combined with the savory goodness of roasted vegetables, creates a plant-based culinary delight. Enjoy the flavors and textures in this dairy-free twist on Alfredo Fotuccini!

Chapter (11) Gluten-Free Alfredo Creations

A. Quinoa Alfredo Fotuccini with Lemon Zest
  1. Catering to Gluten-Sensitive Diets with Alternative Grains:
Ingredients:

- 1 lb gluten-free Fotuccini pasta (quinoa-based or other gluten-free options)
- 1 cup heavy cream
- 1 cup grated Parmesan cheese
- 1/2 cup unsalted butter
- Salt and pepper to taste
- Fresh parsley for garnish
- 2 teaspoons lemon zest
- 1 tablespoon lemon juice

Instructions:

1. Cook gluten-free Fotuccini pasta according to package instructions. Drain and set aside.
2. In a saucepan over medium heat, melt the butter.
3. Pour in the heavy cream, stirring continuously to combine.
4. Gradually add the grated Parmesan cheese, stirring until the sauce is smooth.
5. Season with salt and pepper to taste. Continue stirring until the sauce thickens.
6. Toss the cooked gluten-free Fotuccini pasta into the Alfredo sauce, ensuring an even coating.
7. Add lemon zest and lemon juice, stirring gently to incorporate the citrus flavors.
8. Garnish with fresh parsley before serving.

2. Using Citrus for a Bright and Tangy Twist:

- Lemon zest adds a burst of freshness, and the lemon juice provides a subtle tangy note to complement the richness of the Alfredo sauce.
- Adjust the amount of lemon zest and juice based on personal preference.

This Quinoa Alfredo Fotuccini with Lemon Zest offers a gluten-free alternative using quinoa-based pasta, combining the nuttiness of quinoa with the creamy Alfredo sauce. The addition of lemon zest provides a bright and tangy twist, creating a delightful and gluten-sensitive variation. Enjoy this flavorful and gluten-free Alfredo creation!

Chapter (12) Alfredo Desserts

A. Alfredo Tiramisu

1. Sweetening up the Alfredo Experience with a Dessert Version:
Ingredients:

- 1 cup strong brewed coffee, cooled
- 3 tablespoons coffee liqueur (optional)
- 1 package ladyfinger cookies
- 2 cups vegan or traditional Alfredo sauce
- 1 cup powdered sugar
- 1 teaspoon vanilla extract
- 1 cup vegan or traditional whipped cream
- Cocoa powder for dusting
- Dark chocolate shavings for garnish

Instructions:

1. In a shallow dish, mix the brewed coffee and coffee liqueur (if using).
2. Dip each ladyfinger into the coffee mixture, ensuring they are soaked but not overly soggy.
3. Arrange a layer of soaked ladyfingers in the bottom of a serving dish.
4. In a bowl, combine Alfredo sauce, powdered sugar, and vanilla extract. Mix until smooth.
5. Spread a layer of the Alfredo mixture over the soaked ladyfingers.
6. Repeat the layers until you run out of ladyfingers and Alfredo mixture, ending with a layer of Alfredo on top.
7. Refrigerate the tiramisu for at least 4 hours or overnight to allow the flavors to meld.

8. Before serving, spread a layer of whipped cream on top and dust with cocoa powder.
9. Garnish with dark chocolate shavings for a decadent finish.

2. Layering Flavors for a Delectable Treat:

- Consider adding a hint of cocoa powder or a touch of coffee to the Alfredo mixture for depth of flavor.
- Experiment with different variations such as incorporating a layer of fruit compote between the ladyfingers and Alfredo.

This Alfredo Tiramisu is a sweet twist on the classic savory dish, offering a luscious and indulgent dessert experience. The layers of soaked ladyfingers, creamy Alfredo, and whipped cream create a delectable treat that combines the richness of Alfredo with the beloved flavors of Tiramisu. Enjoy the sweet side of Alfredo!

Chapter (13) Quick and Easy Alfredo Weeknight Dinners

A. One-Pot Alfredo Fotuccini with Broccoli and Sausage

1. Simplifying the Cooking Process for Busy Evenings:

Ingredients:

- 1 lb Fotuccini pasta
- 1 lb Italian sausage, casings removed and crumbled
- 4 cups broccoli florets
- 4 cups chicken broth
- 1 cup heavy cream
- 1 cup grated Parmesan cheese
- 1/2 cup unsalted butter
- Salt and pepper to taste
- Fresh parsley for garnish

Instructions:

1. In a large pot or Dutch oven, brown the crumbled Italian sausage over medium heat until cooked through.
2. Add Fotuccini pasta, broccoli florets, chicken broth, heavy cream, and unsalted butter to the pot.
3. Bring the mixture to a boil, then reduce the heat to simmer.
4. Cook the pasta and broccoli in the simmering liquid, stirring occasionally, until the pasta is al dente and the broccoli is tender-crisp.
5. Once the pasta is cooked, stir in the grated Parmesan cheese until the sauce is smooth and creamy.
6. Season with salt and pepper to taste.
7. Garnish with fresh parsley before serving.

2. Maximizing Flavor with Minimal Effort:

- Opt for pre-chopped broccoli florets and pre-grated Parmesan to save time.
- Choose a high-quality Italian sausage for maximum flavor with minimal seasoning required.
- Customize with your favorite sausage variation or add red pepper flakes for a hint of heat.

This One-Pot Alfredo Fotuccini with Broccoli and Sausage is a quick and easy weeknight dinner solution that doesn't compromise on flavor. The combination of sausage, broccoli, and a creamy Alfredo sauce creates a satisfying and comforting meal with minimal effort. Enjoy a delicious dinner without the fuss!

Chapter (14) Alfredo Fotuccini for Entertaining

A. Gourmet Lobster Alfredo Fotuccini
1. Elevating the Dish for Special Occasions:
Ingredients:

- 1 lb Fotuccini pasta
- 2 lobster tails, shells removed and meat diced
- 1 cup heavy cream
- 1 cup grated Parmesan cheese
- 1/2 cup unsalted butter
- Salt and white pepper to taste
- Zest of one lemon
- 2 tablespoons fresh chives, finely chopped
- 2 tablespoons fresh tarragon, chopped
- Pinch of nutmeg
- Lemon wedges for garnish

Instructions:

1. Cook Fotuccini pasta according to package instructions. Drain and set aside.
2. In a large pan, melt the butter over medium heat.
3. Add diced lobster meat to the pan and sauté until just cooked, about 3-4 minutes.
4. Pour in the heavy cream, stirring continuously to combine.
5. Gradually add the grated Parmesan cheese, stirring until the sauce is smooth.
6. Season with salt, white pepper, and a pinch of nutmeg to taste. Continue stirring until the sauce thickens.
7. Toss the cooked Fotuccini pasta into the Lobster Alfredo sauce,

ensuring an even coating.

8. Sprinkle lemon zest, fresh chives, and chopped tarragon over the pasta.
9. Serve immediately, garnished with additional herbs and lemon wedges.

2. Pairing with Wine and Creating an Elegant Presentation:

- Wine Pairing: Consider pairing this gourmet dish with a crisp Chardonnay or a light Pinot Grigio to complement the richness of the Alfredo and the delicate flavors of lobster.

Elegant Presentation:

- Serve the Lobster Alfredo Fotuccini in individual bowls or on elegant plates for a sophisticated touch.
- Garnish with additional lobster pieces or whole claws for a stunning visual appeal.
- Arrange a side of asparagus spears or steamed green beans for added color and freshness.

This Gourmet Lobster Alfredo Fotuccini is a luxurious and impressive option for entertaining, perfect for special occasions or a romantic dinner. The combination of succulent lobster, creamy Alfredo sauce, and aromatic herbs creates a dish that is both indulgent and memorable. Enjoy the elevated flavors and elegance of this Alfredo creation!

Chapter (15) Historical Alfredo Fotuccini Variations

A. Ancient Roman-Inspired Alfredo Fotuccini with Garum and Pine Nuts

1. Exploring Historical Roots and Culinary Evolution:
Ingredients:

- 1 lb Fotuccini pasta
- 1 cup heavy cream
- 1 cup grated Pecorino Romano cheese
- 1/2 cup unsalted butter
- Salt to taste
- 2 tablespoons garum (fermented fish sauce) or anchovy paste
- 1/4 cup pine nuts, toasted
- Freshly ground black pepper to taste
- Fresh parsley for garnish

Instructions:

1. Cook Fotuccini pasta according to package instructions. Drain and set aside.
2. In a saucepan over medium heat, melt the butter.
3. Pour in the heavy cream, stirring continuously to combine.
4. Gradually add the grated Pecorino Romano cheese, stirring until the sauce is smooth.
5. Season with salt and freshly ground black pepper to taste.
6. Stir in garum or anchovy paste, adjusting the amount to your preferred level of umami.
7. Toss the cooked Fotuccini pasta into the Ancient Roman-inspired Alfredo sauce, ensuring an even coating.
8. Sprinkle toasted pine nuts over the pasta.

9. Garnish with fresh parsley before serving.

2. Adapting Ancient Ingredients for a Modern Palate:

- Garum Substitution: If garum is challenging to find, anchovy paste is a suitable alternative, providing a rich umami flavor.
- Pine Nut Toasting: Toast pine nuts in a dry pan over medium heat until golden brown, enhancing their nutty aroma.

This Ancient Roman-inspired Alfredo Fotuccini with Garum and Pine Nuts offers a glimpse into historical culinary influences, combining traditional Roman ingredients with the modern concept of Alfredo Fotuccini. The use of garum and pine nuts provides a unique and savory twist to this historical variation. Enjoy this exploration of flavors and culinary evolution!

Chapter (16) DIY Alfredo Pasta Shapes

A. Homemade Fettuccine Alfredo

1. Crafting Pasta from Scratch for an Authentic Touch:

Ingredients for Homemade Fettuccine:

- 2 cups all-purpose flour
- 3 large eggs
- Pinch of salt

Ingredients for Alfredo Sauce:

- 1 lb homemade fettuccine pasta
- 1 cup heavy cream
- 1 cup grated Parmesan cheese
- 1/2 cup unsalted butter
- Salt and white pepper to taste
- Fresh parsley for garnish

Instructions for Homemade Fettuccine:

1. On a clean surface, create a mound with the flour and make a well in the center.
2. Crack the eggs into the well and add a pinch of salt.
3. Using a fork, gradually incorporate the flour into the eggs until a dough forms.
4. Knead the dough for about 10 minutes until smooth. Wrap it in plastic wrap and let it rest for 30 minutes.
5. Roll out the dough into a thin sheet and cut it into fettuccine-shaped strips using a pasta cutter or a knife.
6. Cook the homemade fettuccine in boiling salted water for 2-3 minutes until al dente. Drain and set aside.

Instructions for Alfredo Sauce:

1. In a saucepan over medium heat, melt the butter.
2. Pour in the heavy cream, stirring continuously to combine.
3. Gradually add the grated Parmesan cheese, stirring until the sauce is smooth.
4. Season with salt and white pepper to taste.
5. Toss the cooked homemade fettuccine into the Alfredo sauce, ensuring an even coating.
6. Garnish with fresh parsley before serving.

2. Pairing with the Perfect Alfredo Sauce Consistency:

- The homemade fettuccine cooks quickly, so have the Alfredo sauce ready before starting the pasta.
- Reserve a bit of pasta water to adjust the sauce consistency if needed.
- Opt for a slightly thicker Alfredo sauce to cling to the homemade pasta, ensuring a perfect pairing.

Crafting homemade fettuccine for your Alfredo dish adds a personal touch and elevates the dining experience. The combination of fresh pasta and a velvety Alfredo sauce creates an authentic and delightful meal. Enjoy the satisfaction of creating pasta from scratch and savor the delicious flavors!

Chapter (17) Alfredo Fotuccini Across the Regions

A. Northern Italian Alfredo Fotuccini with Porcini Mushrooms
  1. Recognizing Regional Variations and Ingredients:
Ingredients:

- 1 lb Fotuccini pasta
- 1 cup heavy cream
- 1 cup grated Parmesan cheese
- 1/2 cup unsalted butter
- Salt and white pepper to taste
- 1 cup dried porcini mushrooms, rehydrated and sliced
- 2 tablespoons extra virgin olive oil
- 2 cloves garlic, minced
- Fresh thyme leaves for garnish

Instructions:

1. Cook Fotuccini pasta according to package instructions. Drain and set aside.
2. In a skillet over medium heat, add extra virgin olive oil and sauté minced garlic until fragrant.
3. Add rehydrated and sliced porcini mushrooms to the skillet, cooking until they release their moisture and become golden brown.
4. In a saucepan over medium heat, melt the butter.
5. Pour in the heavy cream, stirring continuously to combine.
6. Gradually add the grated Parmesan cheese, stirring until the sauce is smooth.
7. Season with salt and white pepper to taste.
8. Toss the cooked Fotuccini pasta into the Alfredo sauce,

    ensuring an even coating.

9. Add the sautéed porcini mushrooms, gently mixing them into the pasta.
10. Garnish with fresh thyme leaves before serving.

2. Exploring the Diversity within Italian Cuisine:

- Northern Italian cuisine often incorporates butter and cream in pasta dishes, providing a rich and comforting experience.
- Porcini mushrooms, with their earthy and nutty flavor, are a staple in the northern regions of Italy.
- Consider using a high-quality Parmesan or Grana Padano cheese for an authentic touch.

This Northern Italian Alfredo Fotuccini with Porcini Mushrooms showcases the regional flavors and ingredients found in the north of Italy. The combination of creamy Alfredo sauce and the robust taste of porcini mushrooms creates a pasta dish that is both indulgent and rooted in Northern Italian culinary tradition. Enjoy the diverse and delicious offerings of Italian cuisine!

Chapter (18) Healthy Alfredo Fotuccini for Kids

A. Sneaky Veggie Alfredo Mac 'n' Cheese

1. Incorporating Vegetables into a Kid-Friendly Favorite:

Ingredients:

- 1 lb Fotuccini pasta
- 1 cup cauliflower florets
- 1 cup butternut squash, peeled and cubed
- 1 cup carrots, peeled and sliced
- 1 cup milk (whole or 2%)
- 1 cup grated mild cheddar cheese
- 1/2 cup grated Parmesan cheese
- 1/4 cup unsalted butter
- Salt and pepper to taste
- 1/2 teaspoon garlic powder (optional)
- Fresh chives for garnish

Instructions:

1. Cook Fotuccini pasta according to package instructions. Drain and set aside.
2. In a steamer or microwave, steam cauliflower, butternut squash, and carrots until tender.
3. In a blender, combine the steamed vegetables, milk, cheddar cheese, Parmesan cheese, and butter. Blend until smooth.
4. In a saucepan over medium heat, warm the vegetable and cheese mixture, stirring continuously until well combined.
5. Season with salt, pepper, and garlic powder (if using) to taste.
6. Toss the cooked Fotuccini pasta into the Sneaky Veggie Alfredo sauce, ensuring an even coating.

7. Garnish with fresh chives before serving.

2. Tips for Encouraging Young Ones to Enjoy a Nutritious Meal:

- Fun Shapes: Use alphabet or animal-shaped pasta to make the meal more engaging for kids.
- Involve Them: Let kids assist in the vegetable-steaming process or choosing pasta shapes.
- Serve with a Smile: Present the Sneaky Veggie Alfredo Mac 'n' Cheese in a visually appealing way, encouraging kids to enjoy their nutritious meal.

This Sneaky Veggie Alfredo Mac 'n' Cheese provides a wholesome twist to a classic favorite, ensuring kids get their share of vegetables in a delicious and kid-friendly manner. The creamy Alfredo sauce, enriched with hidden veggies, creates a nutritious and comforting dish that will be a hit with both parents and kids alike. Enjoy a healthier take on Alfredo Fotuccini for family meals!

Chapter (19) Alfredo Fotuccini as Comfort Food

A. Slow Cooker Alfredo Fotuccini Casserole

1. Embracing the Warmth and Ease of Slow Cooking:

Ingredients:

- 1 lb Fotuccini pasta
- 2 cups cooked and shredded chicken breast
- 1 cup frozen peas
- 1 cup sliced mushrooms
- 2 cups chicken broth
- 2 cups heavy cream
- 1 cup grated Parmesan cheese
- 1/2 cup unsalted butter, melted
- 1 teaspoon garlic powder
- Salt and pepper to taste
- Fresh parsley for garnish

Instructions:

1. Cook Fotuccini pasta according to package instructions until just undercooked. Drain and set aside.
2. In a large bowl, mix together cooked and shredded chicken, frozen peas, and sliced mushrooms.
3. In a separate bowl, whisk together chicken broth, heavy cream, grated Parmesan cheese, melted butter, garlic powder, salt, and pepper.
4. Place half of the partially cooked Fotuccini pasta in the slow cooker, followed by half of the chicken and vegetable mixture. Pour half of the Alfredo sauce over the layers.
5. Repeat the layering process with the remaining pasta, chicken

mixture, and Alfredo sauce.

6. Cover the slow cooker and cook on low for 2-3 hours or until the pasta is fully cooked and the sauce is creamy.
7. Stir gently to combine all the ingredients.
8. Garnish with fresh parsley before serving.

2. Creating a Comforting Dish for Cozy Nights:

- Slow Cooker Convenience: Utilize the slow cooker to simplify the cooking process and infuse flavors into the Fotuccini.
- Personal Touch: Add your favorite comfort ingredients such as extra cheese or a sprinkle of nutmeg for added warmth.
- Serve Family-Style: Allow everyone to scoop their portion directly from the slow cooker for a cozy and communal dining experience.

This Slow Cooker Alfredo Fotuccini Casserole brings the comfort of slow cooking to a classic pasta dish, creating a creamy and satisfying meal perfect for cozy nights at home. The combination of tender pasta, succulent chicken, and a rich Alfredo sauce makes this casserole a delightful and comforting option for any occasion. Enjoy the warmth and ease of this comforting Alfredo Fotuccini!

Chapter (20) Alfredo Fotuccini on a Budget

A. Economical Alfredo Fotuccini with Pantry Staples

1. Maximizing Flavor with Affordable Ingredients:

Ingredients:

- 1 lb Fotuccini pasta
- 2 cups milk
- 1/2 cup unsalted butter
- 1 cup grated Parmesan cheese
- Salt and black pepper to taste
- 1 teaspoon garlic powder
- 1 tablespoon all-purpose flour (optional, for thickening)
- Fresh parsley for garnish

Instructions:

1. Cook Fotuccini pasta according to package instructions. Drain and set aside.
2. In a saucepan over medium heat, melt the butter.
3. If using flour, sprinkle it over the melted butter and whisk to create a roux. Cook for 1-2 minutes.
4. Gradually whisk in the milk, ensuring there are no lumps.
5. Stir in the grated Parmesan cheese, garlic powder, salt, and black pepper.
6. Continue cooking and stirring until the sauce thickens and the cheese is fully melted.
7. Toss the cooked Fotuccini pasta into the economical Alfredo sauce, ensuring an even coating.
8. Garnish with fresh parsley before serving.

2. Tips for Budget-Friendly Variations and Substitutions:

- Cheese Substitutions: Use a combination of Parmesan and a more affordable cheese like mozzarella or cheddar to maintain flavor while reducing cost.
- Vegetarian Option: Skip the meat additions and focus on affordable vegetables like peas or sautéed spinach for added nutrition.
- Bulk Purchase: Buy Fotuccini pasta and Parmesan cheese in bulk to save on unit costs.

This Economical Alfredo Fotuccini with Pantry Staples demonstrates that a delicious and satisfying meal can be created without breaking the bank. By utilizing budget-friendly ingredients and simple pantry staples, you can enjoy a comforting plate of Alfredo Fotuccini that's light on the wallet. Enjoy a tasty and economical twist on a classic pasta dish!

Chapter (21) The Art of Garnishing Alfredo Fotuccini

A. Herb-Infused Olive Oil Drizzle

1. Elevating Presentation with Simple Garnishes:

Ingredients:

- 1 lb Fotuccini pasta
- 1 cup heavy cream
- 1 cup grated Parmesan cheese
- 1/2 cup unsalted butter
- Salt and white pepper to taste
- Fresh parsley, finely chopped, for garnish
- Herb-infused olive oil (rosemary, thyme, or basil), for drizzling

Instructions:

1. Cook Fotuccini pasta according to package instructions. Drain and set aside.
2. In a saucepan over medium heat, melt the butter.
3. Pour in the heavy cream, stirring continuously to combine.
4. Gradually add the grated Parmesan cheese, stirring until the sauce is smooth.
5. Season with salt and white pepper to taste.
6. Toss the cooked Fotuccini pasta into the Alfredo sauce, ensuring an even coating.
7. Plate the Alfredo Fotuccini and sprinkle with finely chopped fresh parsley.

2. Enhancing Flavors with Infused Oils:

- Herb-Infused Olive Oil: Combine 1/2 cup extra virgin olive oil with a few sprigs of fresh herbs (rosemary, thyme, or basil) in a small saucepan. Heat over low heat for 5-10 minutes to infuse the oil with herb flavors. Strain and cool.
- Drizzling Technique: Using a small spoon, drizzle the herb-infused olive oil over the plated Alfredo Fotuccini in a decorative pattern.

This Herb-Infused Olive Oil Drizzle adds a touch of elegance to your Alfredo Fotuccini, elevating both the presentation and flavor profile. The infusion of herbs into the olive oil introduces additional aromatic notes that complement the richness of the Alfredo sauce. Impress your guests or simply enjoy a restaurant-worthy experience at home with this artful garnish!

Chapter (22) Alfredo Fotuccini for Special Diets

A. Keto-Friendly Alfredo Fotuccini with Zoodles

   1. Adapting the Dish for Low-Carb Diets:

Ingredients:

- 2 large zucchinis (zoodles)
- 1 cup heavy cream
- 1 cup grated Parmesan cheese
- 1/2 cup unsalted butter
- Salt and white pepper to taste
- 2 cloves garlic, minced
- 1 tablespoon olive oil
- Fresh basil for garnish

Instructions:

1. Using a spiralizer, create zucchini noodles (zoodles) from the zucchinis.
2. In a large skillet over medium heat, add olive oil and minced garlic. Sauté until fragrant.
3. Add the zoodles to the skillet and sauté for 2-3 minutes, or until just tender. Remove from heat and set aside.
4. In a saucepan over medium heat, melt the butter.
5. Pour in the heavy cream, stirring continuously to combine.
6. Gradually add the grated Parmesan cheese, stirring until the sauce is smooth.
7. Season with salt and white pepper to taste.
8. Toss the sautéed zoodles into the Alfredo sauce, ensuring an even coating.
9. Serve the Keto-Friendly Alfredo Fotuccini with fresh basil for

garnish.

2. Maintaining the Essence of Alfredo in a Keto-Friendly Version:

- Creamy Texture: The heavy cream and Parmesan cheese combination creates a velvety sauce that mirrors the traditional Alfredo texture.
- Garlic Infusion: Using minced garlic in the sautéing process infuses the dish with classic Alfredo flavors.
- Fresh Herb Garnish: Fresh basil adds a pop of color and a hint of freshness, complementing the richness of the Keto-Friendly Alfredo Fotuccini.

This Keto-Friendly Alfredo Fotuccini with Zoodles offers a low-carb alternative to the classic pasta dish without compromising on flavor or creaminess. By utilizing zucchini noodles and keto-friendly ingredients, you can enjoy a satisfying and indulgent Alfredo experience that aligns with your dietary preferences. Delight in this delicious and health-conscious adaptation of Alfredo Fotuccini!

Chapter (23) Alfredo Fotuccini Tapas

A. Bite-sized Alfredo Fotuccini Bites with Roasted Red Peppers
1. Transforming the Classic into an Appetizer for Gatherings:
Ingredients:

- 1/2 lb Fotuccini pasta
- 1/2 cup heavy cream
- 1/2 cup grated Parmesan cheese
- 1/4 cup unsalted butter
- Salt and white pepper to taste
- 1 cup roasted red peppers, finely diced
- Fresh basil leaves for garnish

Instructions:

1. Cook Fotuccini pasta according to package instructions until just undercooked. Drain and set aside.
2. In a saucepan over medium heat, melt the butter.
3. Pour in the heavy cream, stirring continuously to combine.
4. Gradually add the grated Parmesan cheese, stirring until the sauce is smooth.
5. Season with salt and white pepper to taste.
6. Toss the partially cooked Fotuccini pasta into the Alfredo sauce, ensuring an even coating.
7. Allow the pasta to cool slightly.
8. Form small, bite-sized portions of Alfredo Fotuccini, placing a spoonful on a serving tray.
9. Top each bite with finely diced roasted red peppers.
10. Garnish with fresh basil leaves for a burst of color.

2. Incorporating Bold Flavors in Small, Shareable Portions:

- Roasted Red Peppers: Add a sweet and smoky flavor to each bite, complementing the richness of the Alfredo sauce.
- Bite-sized Portions: Create an interactive and social dining experience with mini forks or toothpicks for easy serving.
- Presentation: Arrange the Alfredo Fotuccini Bites on a stylish platter, showcasing the vibrant colors and inviting your guests to indulge.

These Bite-sized Alfredo Fotuccini Bites with Roasted Red Peppers are a delightful twist on the classic, perfect for entertaining and gatherings. The combination of creamy Alfredo, smoky roasted red peppers, and fresh basil creates a burst of flavors in every bite. Enjoy the sophistication and convenience of these tapas-style Alfredo delights!

Chapter (24) Celebrity Chef Inspired Alfredo

A. Gordon Ramsay's Signature Alfredo Fotuccini
1. Infusing the Dish with the Renowned Chef's Culinary Style:
Ingredients:

- 1 lb Fotuccini pasta
- 1 cup heavy cream
- 1 cup grated Parmesan cheese
- 1/2 cup unsalted butter
- Salt and white pepper to taste
- Zest of one lemon
- Fresh chives, finely chopped, for garnish

Instructions:

1. Cook Fotuccini pasta according to package instructions. Drain and set aside.
2. In a saucepan over medium heat, melt the butter.
3. Pour in the heavy cream, stirring continuously to combine.
4. Gradually add the grated Parmesan cheese, stirring until the sauce is smooth.
5. Season with salt and white pepper to taste.
6. Toss the cooked Fotuccini pasta into the Alfredo sauce, ensuring an even coating.
7. Grate the zest of one lemon directly into the pasta, providing a burst of citrusy freshness.
8. Garnish with finely chopped fresh chives for a pop of color and added flavor.

2. Incorporating Unique Techniques for a Gourmet Twist:

- Lemon Zest Infusion: Gordon Ramsay often incorporates citrus to brighten flavors. The lemon zest adds a zesty note to the Alfredo Fotuccini.
- Finishing Touch: Just before serving, drizzle a touch of extra virgin olive oil over the dish for an extra layer of richness.

Gordon Ramsay's Signature Alfredo Fotuccini brings a touch of gourmet flair to this classic Italian dish. With its silky texture, balanced flavors, and a hint of citrus, this rendition reflects the chef's culinary expertise. Enjoy the culinary journey and savor the gourmet twist inspired by the renowned Gordon Ramsay!

Chapter (25) Alfredo Fotuccini Food Pairings

A. Wine and Alfredo: Perfect Pairings for Every Palate

1. Exploring the World of Wine and Alfredo Combinations:

Classic Alfredo Fotuccini:

Wine Pairing: Chardonnay

Why: The buttery and oaked notes of Chardonnay complement the richness of the Alfredo sauce, creating a harmonious pairing.

Chicken Alfredo Fotuccini:

Wine Pairing: Pinot Grigio

Why: The light and crisp nature of Pinot Grigio balances the savory flavors of the chicken and Alfredo, providing a refreshing contrast.

Shrimp and Spinach Alfredo Fotuccini:

Wine Pairing: Sauvignon Blanc

Why: The bright acidity and herbal notes of Sauvignon Blanc enhance the seafood and greens, creating a lively and well-balanced pairing.

Mushroom and Truffle Oil Alfredo Fotuccini:

Wine Pairing: Barbera

Why: The earthy and robust qualities of Barbera complement the umami from mushrooms and truffle oil, creating a delightful synergy.

Cauliflower Alfredo Fotuccini:

Wine Pairing: Viognier

Why: Viognier's floral and fruity notes add a layer of complexity, enhancing the light and vegetable-based cauliflower Alfredo.

2. Enhancing the Dining Experience with Thoughtful Pairings:

Temperature Matters: Serve white wines slightly chilled to enhance their refreshing qualities.

Consider Red Wines: While white wines are traditional, a light-bodied red, such as Pinot Noir, can provide an interesting contrast, especially with meat-based Alfredo variations.

Experiment with Sparkling Wine: For a festive touch, consider a dry sparkling wine or Prosecco. The effervescence cuts through the richness of Alfredo, cleansing the palate.

Pairing wine with Alfredo Fotuccini adds a layer of sophistication to your dining experience. Experiment with different varietals and discover the nuances that complement the various flavors of this classic Italian dish. Cheers to the perfect harmony of food and wine!

Chapter (26) Alfredo Fotuccini Food Artistry

A. Plate Presentation Techniques for Culinary Aesthetics

1. Elevating the Visual Appeal of Your Alfredo Creations:

Classic Alfredo Fotuccini:

Plate Shape: Serve the Fotuccini in a shallow bowl, allowing the sauce to pool at the bottom for a luxurious presentation.

Fresh Herbs: Sprinkle finely chopped parsley or basil on top for a burst of color.

Chicken Alfredo Fotuccini:

Vertical Stacking: Layer the Fotuccini on the plate and top with sliced chicken breast for a visually appealing stack.

Microgreens: Garnish with a small handful of microgreens for a touch of freshness.

Shrimp and Spinach Alfredo Fotuccini:

Circular Arrangement: Arrange the Fotuccini in a circular pattern on the plate.

Lemon Zest: Grate a bit of lemon zest over the dish for a vibrant and aromatic accent.

Mushroom and Truffle Oil Alfredo Fotuccini:

Spiral Presentation: Create a spiral shape with the Fotuccini on the plate.

Truffle Shavings: If available, shave truffles over the dish for a luxurious touch.

Cauliflower Alfredo Fotuccini:

Colorful Vegetables: Add a pop of color with roasted cherry tomatoes or sautéed bell peppers.

Edible Flowers: Garnish with edible flowers for a whimsical and elegant touch.

2. Tips for Artistic Plating and Garnishing:

Negative Space: Allow some empty space on the plate to create a sense of balance and focus on the dish.

Use Contrasting Colors: Place colorful ingredients strategically to create visual interest and contrast.

Sauces as Art: Drizzle extra Alfredo sauce in artistic patterns around the plate for added flair.

Edible Garnishes: Consider using edible flowers, herb sprigs, or citrus zest for an aesthetic and flavorful touch.

Elevate your Alfredo Fotuccini to a work of art by paying attention to plate presentation. With thoughtful arrangement and garnishing, you can turn a classic pasta dish into a visually stunning masterpiece. Enjoy the artistry of both creating and savoring your culinary creations!

❖ Conclusion

A. Celebrating the Versatility and Timeless Appeal of Alfredo Fotuccini:

Alfredo Fotuccini, with its rich history and sumptuous flavors, stands as a testament to the enduring charm of Italian cuisine. From its humble beginnings to becoming a global favorite, this classic dish has captured the hearts and palates of food enthusiasts worldwide.

B. Encouragement to Explore and Create Personalized Variations:

As we conclude this culinary journey, let the spirit of creativity guide your exploration of Alfredo Fotuccini. The recipes provided are just a starting point – an invitation to experiment, adapt, and infuse your own personal touch. Whether you're a traditionalist or an adventurous home chef, there's endless room for innovation within the world of Alfredo Fotuccini.

C. Final Thoughts and Appreciation for the Italian Culinary Masterpiece:

In the realm of pasta dishes, Alfredo Fotuccini shines as a true masterpiece, showcasing the beauty of simplicity and quality ingredients. Its creamy, indulgent nature has made it a symbol of comfort and celebration. May your kitchen be filled with the aroma of garlic, Parmesan, and pasta, as you savor the joy of preparing and enjoying this timeless Italian treasure.

Buon Appetito!